D

ZOOM IN

Drawing Conclusions and Making Inferences

Curriculum A

TO THE STUDENT

In this book, you will learn how to use the reading strategy called **Drawing Conclusions and Making Inferences**. With your teacher's help, you will practice using this strategy to better understand what you read.

Acknowledgments

Product Development

Product Developer: Dale Lyle
Book Editor: Dale Lyle
Book Writer: Lisa Torrey

Design and Production

Product Designer: Susan Hawk
Cover Designer: Susan Hawk

ISBN 978-0-7609-4907-8
©2009—Curriculum Associates, LLC
North Billerica, MA 01862

SALE

15 14 13 12 11 10 9 8

TABLE OF CONTENTS

Drawing Conclusions and Making Inferences

Using clues and what you already know to figure out information that is not directly stated is called **drawing conclusions and making inferences.**

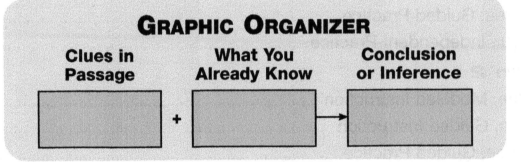

GRAPHIC ORGANIZER

Clues in Passage		What You Already Know		Conclusion or Inference
	+		→	

KEY POINTS

1   Think about information that is **directly stated** as details in the passage. Look for **clues** to information that is not directly stated.

2   Add **what you already know** to the clues in the passage.

3   **Figure out** what is hinted at but not directly stated in the passage.

EXAMPLE

As you read a paragraph, look for **clues** that are directly stated. Then think about **what you already know**. Use the **clues** and **what you already know** to draw a **conclusion** or make an **inference**.

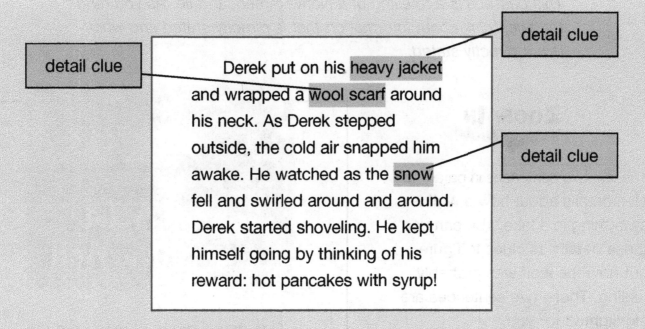

detail clue

detail clue

detail clue

Derek put on his heavy jacket and wrapped a wool scarf around his neck. As Derek stepped outside, the cold air snapped him awake. He watched as the snow fell and swirled around and around. Derek started shoveling. He kept himself going by thinking of his reward: hot pancakes with syrup!

Details tell about people, places, or things. Some details in the paragraph can be used as clues. These details say that Derek is wearing a heavy jacket and wool scarf and that it is snowing. You **already know** that people wear jackets and scarves when it is cold and snowy. The paragraph does not directly state what season of the year it is. But you can use the clues and what you already know to **conclude** that it is winter.

Remember

Use detail clues, along with what you already know, to figure out information that is not directly stated.

Lesson 1, Part One, Modeled Instruction

This passage is a retelling of a Native American tale. As you read the tale, think about information that is directly stated and what is not directly stated.

ZOOM IN

The last two sentences in paragraph 1 give details about how a wolf is swimming in a lake. You can use these details as clues to figure out how the wolf was probably feeling. These two sentences are highlighted for you.

■ *Underline the last two sentences in paragraph 1.*

MY NOTES

A Tale of a Wolf

1   One day, a group of men from the Wolf Clan were fishing in a canoe on a lake. Far away from them, they saw a dark shadow in the water. They paddled quickly toward the shadow, which turned out to be a wolf. The wolf was swimming very slowly, and its tongue was hanging out. The wolf could hardly keep its head above water.

2   The men carefully pulled the wolf out of the water and placed it in their canoe. The wolf opened its eyes, but it did not struggle. The men took the wolf with them back to the village.

3   The wolf lived in the village for many years. Over time, the people in the village began to think of the wolf as a member of their own clan. The wolf hunted with many of the men from the village who had helped to save its life. The wolf could track trails that led the men to deer and other animals. Because of the wolf's help, the people in the village always had plenty of meat to eat and did not go hungry.

4   Years passed, and the wolf grew older. One day, the old wolf curled up on a mat in the front of the clan chief's house. As the sun set, the old wolf died. The people in the village gathered around the dead wolf and bowed their heads. Tears silently fell upon their cheeks.

5   The next night, a man in the village heard a pack of wolves howling. From the dark forest, the wolves' voices rose and fell, as if they were singing a song for one of their own who had died.

The last two sentences in paragraph 4 give details about how people in the village react to the death of the old wolf. You can use these details as clues to figure out how the people in the village were probably feeling. The sentences with the detail clues are highlighted for you.

■   *Underline the last two sentences in paragraph 4.*

MY NOTES

Lesson 1, Part Two, Guided Instruction

This passage is an article. As you read the article, think about information that is directly stated and what is not directly stated.

Egypt's Boy King

ZOOM IN

You can use a detail in the second sentence of paragraph 1 as a clue to figure out why the writer probably decided to title the article "Egypt's Boy King."

■ *Underline the second sentence in paragraph 1.*

MY NOTES

1   One of ancient Egypt's rulers was King Tutankhamun, or King Tut. Tut was only about eight or nine years old when he became king. He ruled Egypt for only ten years, and then he died. No one knows for sure why he died so young.

2   King Tut was buried deep in the Valley of the Kings. This is a place in the desert across from the Nile River. Royal tombs, or graves, were dug deep in the rocky cliffs of the valley to protect them from grave robbers. The people of ancient Egypt believed in life after death. So they buried their dead with food and objects to use in their next life. Some of these objects were very valuable.

3   For over 3,000 years, King Tut's body remained buried deep in its grave. Then, in 1922, a scientist named Howard Carter discovered King Tut's grave. The knot of rope that held together the doors to the grave had not been cut. The clay seal on the doors had not been broken.

4   Howard Carter made a small hole in the corner of the grave's doorway. He lit a candle and put it through the small hole. The flickering flame gave just enough light for Carter to see inside King Tut's grave. What Carter saw left him unable to speak for a few minutes. He saw statues and strange animals. Everything glittered with gold.

5   The discovery of King Tut's tomb, or grave, made news around the world. The grave had four chambers. The chambers were packed with more than 5,000 objects. One of the chambers held a coffin, or chest. King Tut's body was buried inside this chest. The chest weighed almost 250 pounds. 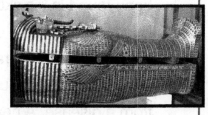 It was made of solid gold.

6   Carter and his team had to work carefully. It took them ten years to take all of the objects out of the grave. They wrote notes about every item. King Tut had used many of the items when he was alive. These items included clothes and jewelry. They also included weapons, chariots, and wooden beds covered in gold. Every object told something about the boy king.

ZOOM IN

You can use details in the fourth sentence of paragraph 4 as clues to figure out how Carter was probably feeling.

■ *Underline the fourth sentence in paragraph 4.*

MY NOTES

The fourth, fifth, and sixth sentences in paragraph 8 give information about the three main ideas about how King Tut died. You can use these details as clues to figure out whether or not scientists probably agree or disagree about how King Tut died.

■ *Underline these three sentences in paragraph 8.*

MY NOTES

7   Many scientists study the past. An important part of their job is to keep exact records. When Carter found King Tut's grave, he wrote many notes in careful detail. Today, new tools and tests have helped scientists find out even more about King Tut. These new tools and tests have also helped scientists find out more about how King Tut died.

8   King Tut's death has always been a mystery. Scientists have wanted to solve this mystery for a long time. There are three main ideas about how King Tut died. Some have thought that a blow to the head killed King Tut, and a piece of bone found in his skull supports this idea. Because of specific clothes and other items found in his grave, others have believed that King Tut suffered and died from a disease. A new test on King Tut's body shows that he may have died from a broken leg that had become diseased.

9   Scientists always use the newest tools of science to study the king's body. And they have been able to rule out one idea about how King Tut died. They now know for sure that he was not killed. They think that the piece of bone found in his skull was broken when he was buried over 3,000 years ago.

10   Scientists have also wondered for a long time what King Tut looked like. They had an idea of what he looked like because artists in ancient Egypt created many statues and wall paintings. Some of these included portraits of King Tut. But scientists still wanted to know what the boy king really looked like. So they did an experiment. They took special pictures of his skull. Then they gave the pictures to three teams of artists. Two of the teams were told where the skull came from, but one team was not told. From the pictures of the skull, each team of artists created a model of King Tut's face.

11   All three teams of artists created models of a face that have very similar features. All three models have the same basic shape of the face. The models show a face with plump cheeks and a round chin. The three models also show similar size and shape of the eyes. All three models have a striking likeness to two ancient portraits. One of these ancient portraits shows King Tut as a child. The other is the gold mask that covered King Tut in his grave.

ZOOM IN

The second sentence in paragraph 10 says that scientists had an idea of what Tut looked like from statues and wall paintings from ancient Egypt. You can use this as a clue to figure out whether or not the images on the statues and wall paintings were realistic.

■   *Underline the second sentence in paragraph 10.*

MY NOTES

You can use details in paragraph 13 as clues to figure out whether or not people in ancient Egypt probably thought that burial preparation was important.

■ *Underline the last eight sentences in paragraph 13.*

MY NOTES

12   People have seen pictures of the models of King Tut's face in the news. People now also have the chance to see King Tut's real face for the first time. In 2007, scientists took the king's body out of the gold coffin, or chest. They put it in a clear case. This is the first time King Tut's body has been on display for people to see. Millions of visitors are expected in Egypt. Not everyone thinks it is a good idea to let the public see the king's body. Some people are worried that large crowds of visitors will damage the body.

13   King Tut's body and face are well preserved. They are well preserved because of how people in ancient Egypt prepared bodies to be buried. First, all organs except for the heart were taken out of the body. These organs were stored in jars. Next, the body was rubbed with salts, minerals, and oils. The body slowly dried out over a few weeks. Only bone, skin, and hair were left. Then the body was wrapped in strips of cloth. The cloth strips were coated with a kind of sticky glue. This protected the body from water damage.

14   In the 1970s, an exhibit about King Tut opened. It displayed 55 of the objects that had been found in King Tut's grave. The exhibit focused on the thrill of Carter's discovery of the grave in 1922. The exhibit was shown in many museums around the world. Millions of people bought tickets. They waited in long lines. For some people, King Tut's treasures were their first glimpse of ancient Egypt. Some of the objects had already become famous. People had seen pictures of them in the news. One of the most famous was a solid gold mask. Bright stones are set into the mask. King Tut was wearing this mask when Carter found his grave.

15   A new exhibit opened in 2007. More than 130 objects went on display. One of the objects was the crown of King Tut. The gold mask was not in the exhibit. It is not allowed to leave Egypt. The exhibit traveled to major museums. Once again, millions of people bought tickets. Many people bought their tickets months ahead of time. This exhibit focused on the time in which King Tut ruled. It also told about the art and the beliefs of the time. Money raised from the exhibit will help build a new museum. It will be built in Egypt.

ZOOM IN

You can use details in the fifth and sixth sentences of paragraph 14 to figure out whether or not people in the 1970s were probably excited to see the exhibit of objects from King Tut's grave.

■ *Underline the fifth and sixth sentences in paragraph 14.*

MY NOTES

This passage is a personal narrative. As you read the personal narrative, think about information that is directly stated and what is not directly stated.

ZOOM IN

The seventh sentence in paragraph 1 says that the two sisters knew many of the stories by heart. The eighth sentence says that they sometimes joined in and told parts of the stories. From these two detail clues, do you think that the narrator and her sister had probably heard their grandmother tell many of the same stories before?

■ *Underline the seventh and eighth sentences in paragraph 1.*

MY NOTES

A Story to Remember

1   When my sister and I were young, our grandmother often told us stories. Many of the stories were about her childhood experiences. She grew up in England a long, long time ago. After my sister and I dressed in our pajamas, we would curl up next to our grandmother's rocking chair. She would get herself settled in her chair. Then she would ask, "What story do you want to hear, girls?" My sister and I knew many of the stories by heart. Sometimes we even joined in and told parts of the stories. Then we'd all laugh.

2   One story, however, would always make us become very quiet. We never helped to tell this story. We listened to every word as if it were for the first time. The story was about our grandmother's voyage to America. To this day, my sister and I are amazed that she lived to tell the story.

3   On April 10, 1912, our grandmother was a passenger on a ship. The ship  was named the *Titanic*. The *Titanic* was a brand new ship. The ship was making its first trip across the ocean. It was going from England to America. It would take many days to cross the vast Atlantic Ocean. The *Titanic* would have to pass through dark, icy waters on its long journey. Only 20 lifeboats were on board the ship. The ship, however, had other safety features. The bottom of the ship was divided into many sections with thick steel doors. If one section started to flood, then the steel doors closed, so water could not flood the rest of the ship.

4   Some people called the *Titanic* a "floating palace." The ship was almost four city blocks long. It was as tall as an eleven-story building. Our grandmother thought her eyes were going to pop out of her head when she first saw the ship! She described how crowds of people lined the shore. They waved flags, and a band played. As the ship slowly pulled out of the harbor, passengers came out on the decks. They waved good-bye to their friends and families. The ship's first voyage had begun.

You can use detail clues in the last two sentences in paragraph 3 to figure out whether or not people probably thought that the *Titanic* could not sink.

■ *Underline the last two sentences in paragraph 3.*

You can use details in the first three sentences of paragraph 4 as clues to figure out whether the *Titanic* was an enormous ship or not.

■ *Underline these detail clues in the first three sentences of paragraph 4.*

MY NOTES

The second sentence in paragraph 5 tells that passengers could be heard speaking more than a dozen different languages. You can use this detail clue to figure out if passengers on the ship were probably from many different countries.

■ *Underline the second sentence in paragraph 5.*

You can use additional detail clues in the third and fourth sentences of paragraph 5 to figure out if passengers on the ship were probably from many different countries.

■ *Underline the third and fourth sentences in paragraph 5.*

MY NOTES

5   The *Titanic* carried 2,200 passengers. On the decks of the ship, passengers could be heard speaking more than a dozen different  languages. Some spoke English. Others spoke French, Italian, German, or another language. Some of the ship's passengers were very rich. In fact, some of them were the richest people in the world. Their tickets had cost a lot of money. The rich passengers stayed in the ship's fancy rooms. These rooms were on the top decks of the ship.

6   Not all of the passengers were rich. Some of them were very poor. Many of these passengers were leaving their homes to make a better life in America. Our grandmother was among those passengers. She was leaving her home in England. She had great hopes about her new life in America. She knew she was lucky to have a job waiting for her. On the ship she quickly met other young people her age. They, too, were on their way to America. Their rooms cost the least amount of money. Many people crowded together in these rooms in the lower levels of the ship.

7   For four days, the *Titanic* sailed on its journey across the ocean. On the night of April 14, the ship neared the coast of Canada. Our grandmother joined other passengers on the deck for a stroll. She could see her breath in the air. Stars sparkled like diamonds in the late night sky. All was calm and quiet.

8   Suddenly, a sailor saw something in the dark. He called out, "Iceberg straight ahead!" But it was too late to turn the huge ship away. The side of the ship scraped  against the iceberg. The captain soon learned of the terrible damage to the ship. Many sections in the bottom of the ship were already flooded with water.

9   Sailors ran to get the few lifeboats ready. Sailors let only women and children get into the lifeboats. Our grandmother was one of them. They were lowered into the icy water. People watched helplessly from the lifeboats. They saw the ship tilt. Then it quickly swung up and pointed to the sky. More than 1,500 passengers were still on board, as the ship slowly slid into the ocean and disappeared.

ZOOM IN

Details in the last three sentences in paragraph 9 tell how the ship tilted, slowly slid into the ocean, and disappeared. From these detail clues, what probably happened to the *Titanic*?

■ *Underline the last three sentences paragraph 9.*

MY NOTES

Choose the correct answer to each question. Fill in the answer bubble.

1. **In paragraph 1, detail clues suggest that**

   Ⓐ the grandmother did not tell stories.
   Ⓑ the grandfather told most of the stories in the family.
   Ⓒ the grandmother did not enjoy telling stories about her childhood.
   Ⓓ the two sisters had heard their grandmother tell many of the same stories before.

3. **In paragraph 4, detail clues suggest that the *Titanic***

   Ⓐ was an enormous ship.
   Ⓑ was a small ship.
   Ⓒ did not draw any crowds as it departed.
   Ⓓ began its first voyage without much fuss.

2. **In paragraph 3, detail clues suggest that**

   Ⓐ the *Titanic* had crossed the ocean many times.
   Ⓑ the *Titanic* could not flood and sink.
   Ⓒ the *Titanic* was not a safe ship.
   Ⓓ the *Titanic* would not have to pass through dangerous waters.

4. **In paragraph 5, detail clues suggest that**

   Ⓐ passengers on the *Titanic* were probably from many different countries.
   Ⓑ all of the passengers were from England.
   Ⓒ all of the passengers were very rich.
   Ⓓ the rich passengers stayed in the worst rooms.

Read why each answer choice is correct or not correct.

1. **Ⓐ not correct**
The first sentence in paragraph 1 says that the grandmother often told stories.

Ⓑ not correct
A grandfather is not mentioned in paragraph 1.

Ⓒ not correct
The sixth sentence in paragraph 1 says that the grandmother asked the girls what story they wanted to hear, so she must have enjoyed telling the stories.

● correct
The seventh and eighth sentences in paragraph 1 say that the two sisters knew many of the stories by heart and joined in telling parts of them, so they must have heard them before.

3. **● correct**
Detail clues in the first three sentences of paragraph 4 describe how enormous, or big, the ship was.

Ⓑ not correct
Details in paragraph 4 suggest that the ship was enormous, not small.

Ⓒ not correct
The fifth sentence in paragraph 4 says that crowds of people lined the shore.

Ⓓ not correct
The sixth, seventh, and eighth sentences in paragraph 4 say that people waved flags, a band played, and passengers came out on the decks to wave good-bye. That means there was quite a "fuss."

2. **Ⓐ not correct**
The fourth sentence in paragraph 3 says that the ship was making its first trip across the ocean.

● correct
The last two sentences in paragraph 3 have detail clues about safety features to protect the ship from flooding and sinking.

Ⓒ not correct
The last two sentences describe the ship's safety features.

Ⓓ not correct
The seventh sentence in paragraph 3 says that the Titanic would have to pass through dark, icy waters.

4. **● correct**
Detail clues in the second and third sentences in paragraph 5 say that more than a dozen languages were spoken, including English, French, Italian, German, and others, so passengers on the ship were probably from many different countries.

Ⓑ not correct
Details suggest that some of the passengers might have been from England, but not all of them.

Ⓒ not correct
The fifth sentence in paragraph 5 says that some of the passengers were very rich.

Ⓓ not correct
Details in the last two sentences in paragraph 5 say that the rich passengers had fancy rooms on the top decks of the ship.

Answer each question. Write each answer on the lines.

5. **Tell how you figured out the answer to question 4. What detail clues did you use to figure out the answer?**

_____

_____

_____

6. **Write a sentence that uses detail clues from the last three sentences in paragraph 9 to tell what probably happened to the *Titanic*.**

_____

_____

_____

7. **Write a short paragraph to summarize the whole personal narrative. Tell only the most important information.**

_____

_____

_____

_____

_____

5. Sample Answer:

You can tell that passengers on the ship were probably from many different countries from detail clues in paragraph 5. The passengers spoke more than a dozen different languages, and some of these languages included English, French, Italian, German, or "another language."

This is a correct answer because it tells how to figure out the answer to question 4 using specific detail clues that suggested passengers on the ship were probably from many different countries.

6. Sample Answer:

After the *Titanic* tilted, slowly slid into the ocean, and disappeared, it probably sank to the bottom of the ocean.

This is a correct answer because this sentence tells what probably happened to the ship based on detail clues in paragraph 9.

7. Sample Answer:

The narrator and her sister listened to their grandmother tell many stories. One story, however, was different from all the others. This story told of the grandmother's voyage on the *Titanic*, which struck an iceberg and sank. The grandmother was lucky to be one of the passengers who survived.

This is a correct answer because it is a short paragraph that tells the most important points of the personal narrative. The paragraph tells in a general way what the whole passage is mostly about.

Lesson 1, Part Four, Independent Practice

This passage is an article. As you read the article, think about information that is directly stated and what is not directly stated.

ZOOM IN

You can use detail clues in the first two sentences of paragraph 1 to figure out what the "twinkling lights" probably are.

■ *Underline the first two sentences in paragraph 1.*

MY NOTES

Look Up!

1   On a clear night, have you ever looked up at the sky? What are the twinkling lights you see? Many people enjoy looking at the night sky. In fact, people have been studying the sky for thousands of years. The sky still holds many mysteries. People can make amazing discoveries, just by looking up!

2   In ancient times, people watched the sky for signs of changing seasons. They saw patterns in the positions and movements of the stars. For example, some groups of stars appeared only in a winter night sky. The people gave names to groups of stars that formed shapes or pictures. They also made up stories to explain the star pictures. The ancient Greeks named many groups of stars. They named them after their gods and heroes. Other people have named star pictures after bears and other animals. Scientists who have studied the patterns also named some of the star pictures. In all, 88 star pictures cover the night sky.

3   One of the most familiar star pictures is called the Big Dipper.  Its seven bright stars form the shape of a large pot with a long handle. Over a hundred years ago, slaves in the South looked to the night sky to find the Big Dipper. They followed the Big Dipper. It led them in the right direction to the North, where they would find freedom.

4   The night sky is filled with star pictures of many different heroes and animals. Some of the stars even form pictures of strange creatures, such as a winged horse and a dragon. The stars of the dragon curl around the North Star. You can see the dragon in its place in the sky every night. Perhaps some people have thought that the dragon is protecting the North Star.

5   Only one of the star pictures is in the shape of a musical instrument—a harp. The harp appears in the summer. It shines high in the night sky. The ancient Greeks believed the harp belonged to a great musician. When the musician played his harp, he was able to tame wild beasts.

ZOOM IN

Details in the last three sentences of paragraph 3 tell about slaves in the South using the Big Dipper. You can use these detail clues to figure out how they used the Big Dipper.

■ *Underline the last three sentences in paragraph 3.*

You can use detail clues in the third and fourth sentences of paragraph 4 to figure out why the author of the article probably wrote, "Perhaps some people have thought that the dragon is protecting the North Star."

■ *Underline the third and fourth sentences in paragraph 4.*

MY NOTES

What detail clues in paragraph 6 suggest that the invention of the telescope helped scientists learn more about space than people in ancient times knew? Look at the third, fourth, and fifth sentences.

- *Underline these sentences in paragraph 6.*

The first sentence in paragraph 6 says that people in ancient times looked at the stars only with their eyes. The third and ninth sentences in paragraph 7 suggest that the space telescope has helped scientists today see what people in ancient times probably never saw in space.

- *Underline the first sentence in paragraph 6 and the third and ninth sentences in paragraph 7.*

MY NOTES

6   People in ancient times looked at the stars with only their eyes. They did not have special tools to help them see far into space. In the 1600s, a scientist in Italy used a new invention to study the skies. It was a telescope. It helped him get a better view of the skies. Since then, much stronger telescopes have been made.

7   One modern telescope has changed the way we look at space. It is very powerful. With this telescope, scientists can see 1,000 times farther into space than people in ancient times could. It is the first space telescope. It is called the *Hubble Space Telescope. Hubble* circles Earth every 97 minutes. It travels 360 miles above Earth. From this position, *Hubble's* camera has taken incredible pictures. Some of these pictures are the first ever to show huge systems of stars. Millions of stars can make up one system. These stars are deep in space. They are billions of years old. Scientists study these images to learn more about space.

8   You don't have to be a scientist, though, to learn about the stars in the sky. You don't need a powerful telescope either. All you really need to get started is patience and curiosity. Pick a clear night. Also, try to find a place away from city lights. Streetlights and lights from nearby houses can blot out the stars by making the sky bright. To record what you see, bring along a notebook, pencil, and flashlight.

9   Under good conditions, you will be able to see thousands of stars in the night sky. Some groups of stars, such as the Big Dipper, will be easy to spot. Once you find the Big Dipper, then you'll probably see the Little Dipper nearby. The shape formed by its seven stars should look familiar to you.

10   When recording notes, be sure to write down the date and time. Making sketches will help you remember what you've seen, too. You can practice by sketching the Moon. With only your eyes, you'll be able to see the dark "seas" on its surface. You'll also be able to see the different phases of the Moon as it circles Earth. There is much to see in the sky. Remember to look up!

ZOOM IN

Details in the fifth and sixth sentences of paragraph 8 can be used as clues to figure out what kind of place you should try to find in order to look at the night sky.

■ *Underline the fifth and sixth sentences in paragraph 8.*

MY NOTES

Choose the correct answer to each question. Fill in the answer bubble.

1. **In paragraph 1, detail clues suggest that the "twinkling lights" are probably**

   Ⓐ sun rays.
   Ⓑ stars.
   Ⓒ holiday decorations.
   Ⓓ fireworks.

3. **In paragraph 4, what is one detail clue that suggests the dragon protects the North Star?**

   Ⓐ The stars of the dragon curl around the North Star.
   Ⓑ The dragon appears in the sky at unexpected times.
   Ⓒ The stars of the dragon are brighter than the North Star.
   Ⓓ The dragon's tail points directly at the North Star.

2. **In paragraph 3, detail clues suggest that slaves used the Big Dipper as**

   Ⓐ a large pot.
   Ⓑ a clock.
   Ⓒ a compass.
   Ⓓ a bright light.

4. **In paragraphs 6 and 7, detail clues suggest that the invention of the telescope**

   Ⓐ helped people in ancient times look more closely at the stars and figure out names for them.
   Ⓑ has been helpful only to today's scientists.
   Ⓒ has helped scientists learn much more about space than people in ancient times knew.
   Ⓓ is no longer valued by scientists.

Answer each question. Write each answer on the lines.

5. **Tell how you figured out the answer to question 4. What detail clues did you use to figure out the answer?**

_____

_____

_____

6. **Write a sentence or two that tells why a location in the countryside might be the best place to see stars in the night sky.**

_____

_____

_____

7. **Write a short paragraph to summarize the article. Tell only the most important information.**

_____

_____

_____

_____

Lesson 2, Part One, Modeled Instruction

This passage is a retelling of a tale. As you read the tale, think about information that is directly stated and what is not directly stated.

ZOOM IN

Details in the last sentence of paragraph 1 can be used as clues to figure out what the condition of the old woman seemed to be at this point in her life. The last sentence has been highlighted for you.

■ *Underline the last sentence in paragraph 1.*

MY NOTES

The Old Woman and the Fox

1   There once was an old woman. Except for her two dogs, she lived alone. Her husband had died, and her children had grown up and moved away. Years ago, the old woman had been plump and strong. Now the old woman's clothes hung loosely on her body, and she needed a walking stick to help support herself.

2   One day, the old woman decided to visit her granddaughter who lived in a village many miles away. The old woman left her home and slowly started walking on her journey. Along the way, she saw a sleek fox with sharp teeth. The fox was hungry, and when he saw the old woman, he licked his lips.

3   The old woman told the fox that she was too thin and bony. She would not be a tasty meal for him. The old woman then told the fox that she was going to visit her granddaughter, who would feed her well. The old woman convinced the fox to wait until she was on her way back home, and then she'd be a much better meal for him.

4   The old woman arrived safely at her granddaughter's home. Her granddaughter gave her a great welcome. Already the air was filled with spices and other wonderful smells coming from the kitchen. Over the next week, the old woman ate many delicious meals. After a few days, her clothes no longer hung loosely on her body.

5   On her journey home, the old woman thought of the fox. When the fox suddenly appeared, he said, "I've been waiting for you, and I'm very hungry!" Just when the fox was about to pounce on the old woman, she called at the top of her voice for her two dogs. They came running over the hill and chased away the fox. The old woman chuckled at how she had tricked the fox twice. She was an old woman, but she was not weak!

ZOOM IN

You can use some details in the third and fourth sentences of paragraph 4 as clues to figure out what the granddaughter did to welcome her grandmother to her home. These sentences have been highlighted for you.

■ *Underline the third and fourth sentences in paragraph 4.*

MY NOTES

This passage is an article. As you read the article, think about information that is directly stated and what is not directly stated.

ZOOM IN

You can use details in the second, third, fourth, and fifth sentences of paragraph 2 as clues to figure out whether or not the journey from Anchorage to Nome was a difficult and dangerous one.

- *Underline the detail clues in the third, fourth, and fifth sentences in paragraph 2.*

MY NOTES

A LIFE OR DEATH RACE

1   In the winter of 1925, an awful disease threatened Nome, Alaska. Young people were at high risk of catching it. They could even die from it. If the disease was not stopped, it could quickly spread. Only one medicine could stop the disease. The medicine was in Anchorage, almost 1,000 miles away from Nome. But Nome was covered in ice. The one airplane that could have flown the medicine to Nome was stored away. People were desperate to get the medicine. But how?

2   Alaska's sled dogs came to the rescue. Teams of sled drivers and their dogs set out on the long journey. They braved bitter cold temperatures. They braved snow and strong winds. They raced across the rugged land to carry the medicine to Nome. They covered the 1,000 mile distance in six days. One sled team reached Nome, and the medicine was safely delivered. Leading the team of sled dogs was a husky by the name of Balto.

3   Balto soon became famous around the world. During the journey, reporters had kept people posted on the progress of the dogsled teams. People were gripped by the reports. They wanted to know about the journey as it unfolded in the far north. People admired Balto for his role as the leader of the dog team that made it to Nome. A statue was built to honor Balto. It stands in Central Park in New York City. Balto died in 1933. He is still remembered today.

4   The 1925 journey to Nome is also still remembered. Since 1973, a dogsled race has been held in its honor. The race is called the Iditarod. It is held each March. The course covers nearly 1,200 miles. Part of it traces the trail used in the 1925 journey to Nome. The Iditarod is a major event in dogsled racing. It can draw more than 100 racing teams. Each driver competes with a team of 12 to 16 dogs. The teams race across very difficult land. They must cross mountain ranges and frozen rivers. They also experience harsh winter weather. The teams spend months getting ready for these tough tests in Alaska's wilderness. The race can take 10 days or more. Many feel it is the adventure of a lifetime.

ZOOM IN

You can use details in the fifth and sixth sentences in paragraph 3 as clues to figure out how people probably felt about Balto.

■ *Underline the fifth and sixth sentences in paragraph 3.*

MY NOTES

Details in the second, third, fourth, and fifth sentences of paragraph 5 can be used as clues to figure out whether or not the health of each dog is carefully checked by doctors during the race.

■ *Underline these sentences in paragraph 5.*

MY NOTES

5   During the Iditarod, the teams stop at 26 places along the route. At these points, doctors check the dogs. They check to make sure each dog is in good health and able to go on with the race. Sometimes a dog may be hurt or not healthy enough to continue. Then the dog is immediately flown out of the wilderness for care. If a dog is tired or injured on the trail, the driver will carry the dog in the sled. Dogs' paws are especially at risk of being hurt. They can 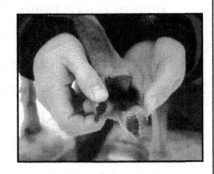 get cuts and sores. Dogsled drivers tie booties onto their dogs' paws. These help to protect the dogs' paws and keep them warm. The booties usually last up to 100 miles. During the race, one driver will use about 2,000 booties for his team of dogs.

6   During the race, the dogs also need rest and plenty of food. Sled dogs can eat almost ten times as much food as normal dogs do. Dogs running the Iditarod need this much food for energy. Extra food is provided at the places along the route where doctors check the dogs. Even with eating all this food, most good sled dogs are not large dogs. Most of them usually weigh less than 55 pounds.

7   So what
makes a good
sled dog?
Many of the
best sled dogs
are huskies.
Huskies are
northern dogs

of mixed breed, or type. The Alaskan
husky, for example, is not a pure breed
of dog. The Siberian husky, however, is
a pure breed of dog. Siberian huskies
usually have blue eyes. Huskies who
race in the Iditarod, though, are not
selected for how they look. They are
selected for how they perform. The best
huskies are born with the desire to pull.
They are also born with strong curiosity.
This curiosity gives them the drive to
see what is down the next road or
around the next corner. One musher, or
sled driver, describes them as wanting
"to be always on the go."

8   Good sled dogs have other special
qualities. They have a quick way of
walking that does not waste any effort.
Because of their smaller size, blood
and oxygen can flow more easily to
their heart, lungs, and muscles. They
also have surprising strength for their
smaller size. One small sled dog can
pull hundreds of pounds of weight.

ZOOM IN

You can use details in the ninth and
tenth sentences in paragraph 7 as
clues to figure out whether or not
the best huskies could be described
as having a unique "attitude."

■ *Underline the ninth and tenth
sentences in paragraph 7.*

MY NOTES

The fifth and sixth sentences in paragraph 10 have details about the relationship of the dogs and their musher. You can use these details to figure out whether or not the dogs want to please the musher.

■ *Underline the fifth and sixth sentences in paragraph 10.*

MY NOTES

9   It takes months of training to teach a group of dogs to work as a team. Each dog has the desire to pull. The dogs, however, need to learn how to pull a sled together as a team. When it is not the winter season, some drivers will use ATVs or wheeled carts instead of sleds to train their teams. They'll rope their teams to the ATVs or carts and let them practice pulling as a team along dirt roads. The top teams spend all year preparing for the race. All this hard work pays off during the race, when carefully trained teams break away into the lead.

10   The top racing teams have strong, fast, and healthy dogs. Careful training helps to create the top teams in the Iditarod. The top teams also have something else that helps them during the race. They have a special bond between the musher, or driver, and his or her dogs. The dogs can read the emotions of the musher. So, if the musher is encouraging, then the dogs respond by working even harder. The bond between a musher and his or her lead dog is especially important. The lead dog is driven by the musher's spoken commands. The lead dog must understand what the musher tells him. The lead dog must also guide the other dogs to do what the musher wants.

11   Many young people want to become mushers. They dream of racing their own dog team in the Iditarod some day. Since 1978, the Jr. Iditarod race has been helping young people gain the experience they will need. The event takes place the weekend before the Iditarod. The junior race is 160 miles in length. Each musher must be between fourteen and seventeen years old. Each team must have between five and ten dogs.

12   The Jr. Iditarod trail is clearly marked. Pilots fly over the trail and report on the progress of all the teams. The teams also stop at places along the trail. At one point, they must stay over for eight to twelve hours. This gives the young mushers the experience of camping in the winter wilderness with their dogs.

13   Many awards and prizes are given after the race. The winner receives money for school. The top placing rookie, or first-time musher, also gets an award. A special award also goes to the most outstanding lead dog.

ZOOM IN

The first two sentences in paragraph 11 give details about young mushers, which you can use as clues to figure out whether or not the interest of young people will help the Iditarod race continue for many years to come.

■ *Underline the first two sentences in paragraph 11.*

MY NOTES

This passage is a story. As you read the story, think about information that is directly stated and what is not directly stated.

ZOOM IN

Details in the fourth, fifth, sixth, and seventh sentences of paragraph 1 provide clues to where Max and Sara live.

■ *Underline the fourth, fifth, sixth, and seventh sentences in paragraph 1.*

MY NOTES

Feathered Friends

1   Max opened a window in the living room. He leaned on the wooden ledge to take a look outside. It was another bright sunny morning. Max heard the sound of cars honking in the street three stories below. Many people carried briefcases. They walked quickly on the crowded sidewalks to nearby subway stations. Some people waved, trying to flag down taxis. Suddenly, Mrs. Kramer's head popped out from the window next door. She waved and shouted good morning to Max. Then she shook out a dust cloth and disappeared back inside the building. Max's sister, Sara, joined him at the window. She squeezed her elbows next to his on the ledge.

2   While watching the morning rush in the street below, Max and Sara decided that they should go to the neighborhood pet shop. They needed to buy seed and other supplies for their birds. Max and Sara raised small songbirds called society finches.

3   Max and Sara told their mother they'd be home in about an hour. Then they walked the familiar route of four blocks to the pet store, "Wings and Chirps." As they walked into the store, a bell jangled on the door, and Mr. Mackey came out from the back room. Mr. Mackey smiled when he saw Max and Sara. He asked how their finches were doing.

Mr. Mackey told them that he had a new shipment of fresh millet seed that the finches would especially enjoy. He packed the long stems of millet in a paper bag. Then he helped Max and Sara collect their usual supply of finch seed. Max and Sara picked out a new birdbath. It would be a special treat for their finches.

4   Sara asked Mr. Mackey if he knew where society finches came from. He said that they were most likely bred in China in the 1700s. He also explained that society finches were related to many other kinds of finches. However, they were the tamest and most social of all finches.

ZOOM IN

You can use one detail in the second sentence of paragraph 3 as a clue to figure out what the pet store probably specialized in.

■ *Circle this detail clue in the second sentence of paragraph 3.*

You can use details in the fourth, fifth, and eighth sentences of paragraph 3 as clues to figure out whether or not Max and Sara were probably regular customers at the store.

■ *Underline the fourth, fifth, and eighth sentences in paragraph 3.*

MY NOTES

Details in the third, ninth, and eleventh sentences in paragraph 5 tell about the colors of Max and Sara's society finches, which you can use as clues to figure out whether or not society finches probably come in a variety of colors.

■ *Underline these sentences in paragraph 5.*

The second sentence in paragraph 5 directly states that Max and Sara easily recognized each finch. Detail clues in the sentences that you have already underlined tell what color each bird was. Might Max and Sara have used color to recognize each bird?

■ *In the sentences that you have underlined in paragraph 5, circle the details that tell the color of each bird.*

MY NOTES

5   When Max and Sara returned home, they checked on their society finches. They easily recognized each finch. Fred was a chocolate brown male. When he sang, usually with great enthusiasm, he would bounce back and forth on the perch. Max tied the stem of millet to the inside of the large, open cage. Sara cleaned the water and seed cups under the watchful eye of Sherlock. Sherlock was their detective. He observed everything very carefully. His feathers were brown and gray. Waiting at the far corner of the cage was their shy and quiet Sweetheart. Her feathers were pale gray. After Max and Sara finished cleaning the cage, Sweetheart joined Fred on the perch.

6   Max and Sara cleaned the birdcage every day. They also cleaned out the water cup many times a day. They always made sure the finches had clean, cool water to drink. It was also important to empty the seed cup and replace it with fresh seed every day.

7   Sara filled the new birdbath to the brim with clean water and placed it on the bottom of the birdcage. Fred immediately began singing again, bouncing back and forth on the perch. Sherlock swooped down and happily pecked the side of the small, blue plastic pool. Then he began singing and bouncing. The usually shy Sweetheart quickly claimed a place on the edge of the birdbath. She dipped her beak into the water, and then she jumped into the water. She lowered her small body down into the water and began to flap her wings. Fred and Sherlock joined  her. The three of them flapped and splashed in the water together. Soon, not a drop of water was left!

8   After bath time, all three of the wet finches perched together and flapped their wings. While they did this, they puffed out the feathers on their bodies. Droplets of water flew off their bodies. Max and Sara laughed. By the time the finches were done flapping, Max and Sara felt as if they had taken a bath, too!

ZOOM IN

Details in paragraph 7 can be used as clues to figure out whether or not the society finches probably enjoyed taking a bath.

■ *Underline the last nine sentences in paragraph 7.*

MY NOTES

Choose the correct answer to each question. Fill in the answer bubble.

1. **Detail clues suggest that Max and Sara live**

   Ⓐ in a big farmhouse.
   Ⓑ in a city.
   Ⓒ in a very small town.
   Ⓓ in the country.

3. **In paragraph 3, detail clues suggest that Max and Sara were probably**

   Ⓐ new customers at the pet store.
   Ⓑ unfamiliar to Mr. Mackey.
   Ⓒ not welcome at the pet store.
   Ⓓ regular customers at the pet store.

2. **From the name "Wings and Chirps" you can figure out that the pet store probably specialized in**

   Ⓐ kittens.
   Ⓑ puppies.
   Ⓒ snakes.
   Ⓓ birds.

4. **In paragraph 5, detail clues suggest that society finches**

   Ⓐ are unfriendly.
   Ⓑ are all the same color.
   Ⓒ come in a variety of colors.
   Ⓓ have different marks on their wings.

Read why each answer choice is correct or not correct.

1. Ⓐ **not correct**

A farmhouse is not mentioned in the story.

● **correct**

The fourth, fifth, sixth, and seventh sentences of paragraph 1 have detail clues about many things that are found in a city, such as honking cars, people carrying briefcases, crowded sidewalks, subway stations, and taxis.

Ⓒ **not correct**

The details in the story do not include things that are specifically found in a very small town.

Ⓓ **not correct**

Things that are usually found in the country are not mentioned in the story.

2. Ⓐ **not correct**

Kittens do not have wings, and they do not chirp.

Ⓑ **not correct**

Puppies do not have wings, and they do not chirp.

Ⓒ **not correct**

Snakes do not have wings, and they do not chirp.

● **correct**

Birds have wings, and they chirp, so the name of the store suggests that the pet store specialized in birds.

3. Ⓐ **not correct**

The second sentence in paragraph 3 says that they walked the familiar route to the pet store, so they were not new customers.

Ⓑ **not correct**

Details in the fifth and eighth sentences suggest that Max and Sara were familiar to Mr. Mackey.

Ⓒ **not correct**

The fourth sentence in paragraph 3 says that Mr. Mackey smiled when he saw Max and Sara, which suggests they were welcome at the pet store.

● **correct**

Detail clues in the fourth, fifth, and eighth sentences in paragraph 3 suggest that Max and Sara were regular customers at the pet store.

4. Ⓐ **not correct**

Details in paragraph 5 do not suggest that society finches are unfriendly, but details in the fourth sentence suggest that Fred is probably friendly.

Ⓑ **not correct**

Details describe the different colors of each of the society finches, so they are not all the same color.

● **correct**

Detail clues describe the different colors of each of Max and Sara's society finches, therefore they come in a variety of colors.

Ⓓ **not correct**

Marks on the finches' wings are not mentioned.

Answer each question. Write each answer on the lines.

5. **Tell how you figured out the answer to question 4. What detail clues did you use to figure out the answer?**

_____

_____

_____

6. **Write two or three sentences that use detail clues from paragraph 7 to tell whether Max and Sara's society finches enjoyed taking a bath.**

_____

_____

_____

7. **Write a short paragraph to summarize the whole story. Tell only the most important information.**

_____

_____

_____

_____

_____

5. Sample Answer:

You can figure out that society finches probably come in a variety of colors because of the detail clues that described the colors of each of Max and Sara's finches. Each society finch had different colored feathers.

This is a correct answer because it tells how to figure out the answer to question 4 using specific detail clues that suggested society finches probably come in a variety of colors.

6. Sample Answer:

Max and Sara's society finches probably enjoyed taking a bath because both Fred and Sherlock sang and bounced, and Sweetheart was not shy about quickly dipping her beak into the water and jumping in. All three flapped their wings and splashed in the water until not a drop was left.

This is a correct answer because these sentences tell that the finches probably enjoyed taking a bath based on detail clues in paragraph 7.

7. Sample Answer:

Max and his sister Sara had three society finches. Each finch was different in color and personality, or character. Max and Sara took very good care of their finches. They visited Mr. Mackey's pet store, where they learned more about the finches and bought their supplies.

This is a correct answer because it is a short paragraph that tells the most important points of the story. The paragraph tells in a general way what the whole passage is mostly about.

Lesson 2, Part Four, Independent Practice

This passage is a report. As you read the report, think about information that is directly stated and what is not directly stated.

ZOOM IN

Look at the seventh, eighth, and ninth sentences in paragraph 1. You can use detail clues in these three sentences to figure out whether or not knights probably had a variety of skills.

■ *Underline the seventh, eighth, and ninth sentences in paragraph 1.*

MY NOTES

Knights of the Middle Ages

1   Knights were important during the Middle Ages, a time period from about 500 to 1500. There were many wars during this time. Different groups of people fought over land and power throughout Europe. People needed to be protected. Knights were warriors who fought on horseback. They usually served a local lord. Knights were highly skilled at riding horses. Knights were also skilled at fighting and using many kinds of weapons. Some knights could also write songs, dance, and draw. The best knights were known far and wide for their skills.

Early Training

2   If a boy was going to become a knight, his training began at a young age. At the age of seven, the boy was sent to live with the lord of a noble family. Many lords were very powerful and had a lot of land and wealth. At the lord's house, the young boy learned many different skills. To begin, he had to learn how to ride a horse and how to behave.

Becoming a Knight

3   At age 14, the young man continued his training by becoming an apprentice to a knight. While working for the knight, the young man learned how to use weapons and how to take care of the knight's armor and horses. He also went into battle with the knight. He learned how to dress the knight in armor. He also had to learn how to help if the knight was hurt or thrown from his horse. When not in battle, the young man practiced his skills with other young men who wanted to become knights. They trained together to improve their strength and to keep in shape for fighting. They trained by wrestling, throwing stones, and fighting with swords.

If the young man learned these skills successfully, he became a knight around the age of 21. A special ceremony was held. Sometimes, a king performed the ceremony. After the ceremony, a celebration was held, and the knight showed off his skills.

ZOOM IN

From detail clues in the first and ninth sentences of paragraph 3 you can figure out whether or not it probably took many years for a young man to become a knight.

■ *Underline these detail clues in the first and ninth sentences in paragraph 3.*

You can use detail clues in the last three sentences in paragraph 3 to figure out whether or not it was an important occasion when a young man became a knight.

■ *Underline the last three sentences in paragraph 3.*

MY NOTES

You can use details in the first three sentences of paragraph 4 as clues to figure out whether or not a knight's weapons were probably dangerous.

■ *Underline the first three sentences in paragraph 4.*

Look at the fourth sentence in paragraph 4, along with the first three sentences. Were knights probably trying to protect themselves from dangerous weapons?

■ *Underline the fourth sentence in paragraph 4.*

MY NOTES

Weapons, Armor, and Horses

4   A knight's most important weapon was his sword. When fighting on horseback, a knight also used a type of spear called a lance. These weapons were very sharp. To protect themselves during battle, knights began wearing full suits of metal armor by the 1400s. The surface of the armor was smooth. During battle, the point of an enemy's weapon slid off the smooth surface of a knight's armor. Armor didn't completely protect knights from harm, however. As more knights wore armor, swords were made with even sharper points. These swords could pierce through the gaps between the metal plates of the armor.

5   Horses were also an important part of a knight's equipment. They were needed for war. They were also needed for hunting, traveling, and carrying bags. Horses were expensive, though. The most expensive horse was the one a knight took into battle. Only a rich knight could afford to buy armor for his battle horse.

At the Castle

6   Knights often lived in their lord's castle. They protected the castle from attack. They also protected the lord's vast area of land. The lord usually owned many large houses and farms on the land. Knights were not always away at war or busy protecting the castle. During times of peace, everyone gathered in the castle's great hall. Everyone ate meals together in the great hall. Music was usually played during meals. Dancing was also welcomed as entertainment during meals. To help pass long evenings at the castle, people also played board games.

7   A knight's family also lived at the castle. If a knight had sons, his oldest son would become a knight, too. Like his father, he would begin his early training around the age of seven. When a knight died, his oldest son received his coat of arms, or shield. Symbols and colors painted on the shield named the knight.

ZOOM IN

Details in the eighth and ninth sentences in paragraph 6 can be used as clues to figure out whether or not meals in the great hall were probably enjoyable occasions.

■ *Circle these detail clues in the eighth and ninth sentences in paragraph 6.*

MY NOTES

Choose the correct answer to each question. Fill in the answer bubble.

1. **What do detail clues suggest about knights?**

   Ⓐ They had a variety of skills.
   Ⓑ They lived a long life.
   Ⓒ They had a great deal of wealth.
   Ⓓ They were local lords.

2. **Detail clues in paragraph 3 suggest that before a young man became a knight, he had to**

   Ⓐ kill a dragon.
   Ⓑ serve the king.
   Ⓒ train for many years.
   Ⓓ win a horse-riding contest.

3. **Detail clues suggest that when a young man became a knight, it was probably**

   Ⓐ an important occasion.
   Ⓑ an everyday event.
   Ⓒ an unhappy moment.
   Ⓓ an unimportant event.

4. **In paragraph 4, detail clues suggest that the weapons knights used in battle were**

   Ⓐ useless.
   Ⓑ dangerous.
   Ⓒ very well-made.
   Ⓓ for decoration only.

Answer each question. Write each answer on the lines.

5. **Tell how you figured out the answer to question 4. What detail clues did you use to figure out the answer?**

_____

_____

_____

6. **Write a sentence that tells why meals in the great hall were probably enjoyable occasions.**

_____

_____

_____

7. **Write a short paragraph to summarize the report. Tell only the most important information.**

_____

_____

_____

_____

Lesson 3, Part One, Modeled Instruction

This passage is an article. As you read the article, think about information that is directly stated and what is not directly stated.

ZOOM IN

You can use details in the first two sentences of paragraph 1 as clues to figure out whether or not ladybugs probably have three pairs of jointed legs. These two sentences are highlighted for you.

■ *Underline the first two sentences in paragraph 1.*

MY NOTES

Ladybugs

1   Ladybugs are small insects. Insects have three pairs of jointed legs. Insects usually have two pairs of wings. Their bodies are divided into three parts. Ladybugs are most often red with black spots. However, some ladybugs are black with red spots. There are about 5,000 different types of ladybugs in the world. Each type of ladybug can be recognized by the number of spots it has. One common type of ladybug is red with two black spots. As ladybugs get older, their spots fade.

2   Ladybugs eat aphids. In fact, aphids are their favorite food. Aphids are tiny bugs that eat plants. Aphids can destroy a farmer's crops and a gardener's plants. One ladybug can eat as many as 50 aphids a day.

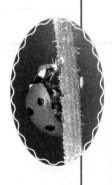

3   Many birds and insects eat ladybugs. To protect themselves, ladybugs do what some other animals do. They pull their legs inside their body and stay very still. They also give off a bad smell. When they feel safe, ladybugs go on with their usual activities. Another way ladybugs protect themselves is by color. The colors red and black are a warning sign. The colors warn birds and insects of danger. The colors also warn that the ladybug might not be a tasty meal.

4   Ladybugs have been a symbol of good luck for a long time. To people in England, finding a ladybug means a good harvest. To people in France, finding a ladybug means an illness might be cured. To others, finding a ladybug in the house in winter means good luck. Some people even count a ladybug's spots. They hope this will tell them what the future holds.

ZOOM IN

The second and third sentences in paragraph 3 have details that you can use as clues to figure out what a ladybug would probably be trying to do if it pulled its legs inside its body and stayed very still. These sentences are highlighted for you.

■ *Underline the second and third sentences in paragraph 3.*

MY NOTES

This passage is an article. As you read the article, think about information that is directly stated and what is not directly stated.

ZOOM IN

You can use details in the third, fourth, fifth, sixth, and seventh sentences in paragraph 1 as clues to figure out whether or not the Alps can be a dangerous place to hike.

■ *Underline these sentences in paragraph 1.*

MY NOTES

Frozen in Time

1   One day in 1991, two German tourists were hiking in the Alps near the border of Austria and Italy. The Alps are a high mountain range in Europe. Usually, there is a lot of snow on the ground. The trails are steep and rocky. Storms can move in quickly and surprise even the most experienced hikers. Sometimes hikers become lost or hurt in the Alps. Sometimes they die.

2   As the two tourists hiked in the Alps, they suddenly saw something sticking out of the snow and ice. What was it? As they looked more closely, they realized it was a human body! The skeleton lay half buried in the snow and ice, with the skull facing downward.

3   The tourists hurried to a hikers' shelter to report what they had found. At the shelter, the police were called to come get the body. However, the police could not come for many days. Meanwhile, other hikers and mountain climbers began to hear about the body frozen in the ice. Many came to see the body for themselves. Could it be the body of a hiker?

4   One famous mountain climber, Reinhold Messner, was among the many people who came to see the body frozen in the ice. Messner looked very carefully at the body, but he did not disturb it. The skin on the body was brown and dry and looked like leather. Scattered around the body were pieces of carved wood. Messner thought these pieces of wood looked like tools.

5   The police decided to call an expert for help with the body. Dr. Henn was a special doctor. He examined dead bodies to figure out how they had died. Dr. Henn had examined hundreds of dead bodies, but he had never seen a body like this before. It was a mummy! A mummy is a body that has been preserved, or kept as close as possible to the way it was when it was alive. This mummy had been preserved in the snow and ice.

6   Dr. Henn and an assistant carefully removed the mummy from the ice. When they finally freed the mummy from the ice, they saw that he was still wearing a shoe made of grass on his left foot. They found a tool belt around his waist. On the belt was a knife with a wooden handle. The knife had a small blade made of stone. This was not a modern tool. This was a kind of tool people used thousands of years ago.

ZOOM IN

You can use a detail in the second sentence of paragraph 6 as a clue to figure out whether or not the mummy was the body of a hiker from modern times.

■ *In the second sentence of paragraph 6, underline the four words that tell this detail clue.*

MY NOTES

Two details in the sixth and eighth sentences in paragraph 8 can be used as clues to figure out whether or not the clothing of the Iceman had probably been made well.

■ *Underline the two detail clues in the sixth and eighth sentences in paragraph 8.*

MY NOTES

7   Dr. Henn took the body of the frozen man to the medical school where he worked. Many people, including reporters, wanted to see the mummy. Reporters had even given the mummy a nickname. They called him the Iceman. Dr. Henn and his team put the Iceman into a large, cold room that was like a big refrigerator. Other scientists came to look at the mummy. These included Dr. Spindler, an expert in ancient people. He was most excited about seeing the objects that had been found with the Iceman. He studied ancient objects in order to learn more about the people who made and used them.

8   Clothing and many other objects were found near the place where the mummy was first discovered. The clothing included a fur cap and a piece of the bottom of one of his shoes. Shredded parts of a coat and cape were also found. Both items were damaged when recovering them from the snow and ice. The Iceman's coat was made from deer and wild goat skin. The coat had neatly sewn seams. It also had a few worn places that had been roughly stitched back together with grass threads. The cape was made from skillfully woven grass.

9   A box made from birch tree bark was among the objects found with the Iceman. Inside the birch box were pieces of burned wood. They were wrapped in maple leaves. Scientists think the Iceman used these pieces of burned wood as coals for building a fire. Scientists figured out that the coals in the box were from two different kinds of wood. One kind of wood grows only high up in the mountains. The other kind of wood grows only in the valleys.

10   The Iceman's bow and arrows were also found with him. The bow was nearly six feet long and made from yew wood, which is strong and able to bend easily without breaking. A bow this large would have been powerful enough to hunt animals such as deer and wild goats. A quiver, or case for arrows, was also found with the Iceman. The quiver was made of deerskin and contained twelve arrows.

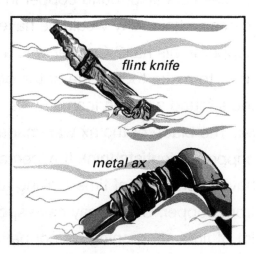

flint knife

metal ax

You can use details in the first four sentences of paragraph 9 as clues to figure out whether or not the Iceman used materials in nature to make what he needed.

■ *Underline these detail clues in the first four sentences in paragraph 9.*

MY NOTES

Details in the third and fifth sentences of paragraph 11 can help you figure out when the Iceman lived. Was it probably during the late Stone Age?

■ *Underline the third and fifth sentences in paragraph 11.*

11   Scientists used a special test to figure out how old the Iceman was. This test can tell the age of almost anything that ever lived. The test showed that the Iceman was 5,300 years old. Experts in history have given names to different periods of time. The period of time that took place over 5,000 years ago is known as the late Stone Age.

12   Scientists used all kinds of clues to find out more about the Iceman and his life. Small bits of wheat and other grains were found stuck in the Iceman's clothing. The Iceman's teeth were worn down. Scientists think his teeth might have been worn from chewing on sand. Sand was often accidentally mixed with wheat. This happened when the grain was ground into flour.

13   Scientists also found copper in the Iceman's hair. Why would he have copper in his hair? Copper was a metal used to make tools. One of the other tools found with the Iceman was an ax. The blade of the ax was made from copper. Scientists think the Iceman may have spent a lot of time making tools from copper. Or, he may have spent a lot of time sharpening his copper ax.

14   Over the years, more than 100 scientists have studied the Iceman. They all studied the Iceman's body and the objects found with him in order to learn more about his life. They also studied the body and objects in order to find out how the Iceman died. Scientists have different ideas about how he died. He could have been caught in a sudden storm. He could have been hurt while hunting animals. He could have been running from an enemy.

15   Scientists also wanted to know how the Iceman's body became a mummy. To become a mummy, his body would have had to dry out. But under the snow and ice, how could his body have dried out? Usually, the Alps are very cold. Every now and then, though, the Alps are a little bit warmer. Some scientists think that snow was blown off the Iceman's body by a warm wind. Then the warm wind dried out the body, and it became a mummy. Other scientists think the Iceman's body was always under snow and ice. They think that under the frozen snow and ice, the body could have dried out. Scientists still have much to learn!

ZOOM IN

You can use details in the fourth, fifth, sixth, and seventh sentences in paragraph 14 as clues to figure out whether or not scientists know for sure how the Iceman died.

■ *Underline the fourth, fifth, sixth, and seventh sentences in paragraph 14.*

MY NOTES

Lesson 3, Part Three, Guided Practice

This passage is a story. As you read the story, think about information that is directly stated and what is not directly stated.

ZOOM IN

From detail clues in the first three sentences of paragraph 1, do you think that Frankie is probably feeling hot and thirsty?

■ *Underline the first three sentences in paragraph 1.*

MY NOTES

The Tomatoes Time Forgot

1   Frankie wiped the sweat off his forehead with the back of his hand. His mouth felt like a wad of dry cotton. He longed for a sip of cool water. Insects circled Frankie's head, but Frankie had given up swatting at them. As Frankie bent down to weed another row of beans, he couldn't understand why his grandfather enjoyed keeping a garden. As far as Frankie was concerned, a garden was too much work. Still, he had promised his grandfather that he would help with the weeding. He didn't want to disappoint his grandfather.

2   To Frankie's surprise, his grandfather was inside taking a nap. It wasn't like his grandfather to trust the garden to someone else. Frankie's grandfather had been feeling tired the last few days. Frankie hoped his grandfather wasn't ill. Working alone in the garden without his grandfather just wasn't the same. To keep his mind off his grandfather, Frankie finished weeding the beans. Then he turned his attention to the tomatoes.

3   The tomatoes were the pride and joy of the garden. Frankie worked carefully as he weeded around the base of each plant. He loved the names  of each type—big rainbow, green zebra, golden sunray, and Caspian pink. They were old types of tomatoes. The seeds from each type had been passed down over many years. Frankie's grandfather had told him about each one. Frankie's grandfather told him that the Caspian pink was first grown in Russia! Frankie thought it was cool how the names of the plants described what the tomatoes looked like.

4   Frankie's grandmother brought out a pitcher of lemonade. Frankie set down the hoe and joined his grandmother. They sat at a small table underneath the shade of the maple tree. She poured Frankie a tall glass of lemonade with ice, and he drank it in one long gulp. She said the garden looked very nice. As she said this, she softly patted Frankie's hand. "Don't worry," she said. "Your grandfather's going to be fine. He'll perk up as soon as he sees what a good job you've done with the tomatoes."

You can use four details in the third sentence of paragraph 3 as clues to figure out whether or not the grandfather probably grew a variety of tomatoes.

■   *Underline these four detail clues in the third sentence of paragraph 3.*

You can use details in the last three sentences in paragraph 4 to figure out whether or not Frankie's grandmother is probably trying to reassure him, or ease his worries and fears, about his grandfather.

■   *Underline the last three sentences in paragraph 4.*

MY NOTES

In the fourth sentence of paragraph 5, the grandfather said he didn't want Frankie upsetting the tomatoes. You can use two details in the fifth sentence as clues to figure out if the grandfather was teasing Frankie.

■ *Underline these two detail clues in the fifth sentence of paragraph 5.*

What detail in the sixth sentence of paragraph 5 can you use as an additional clue to figure out whether Frankie's grandfather was probably teasing him?

■ *Underline this detail clue in the sixth sentence in paragraph 5.*

MY NOTES

5   The screen door opened, and Frankie's grandfather walked toward them. Frankie jumped up and ran to him to help, but his grandfather waved him away. "I hear you've been weeding the garden, so I thought I'd better come out and take a look. I don't want you to be upsetting the tomatoes." As the grandfather spoke, his eyes sparkled, and he winked at Frankie. He flashed Frankie a big smile and said, "Let's see if you've learned anything about gardening."

6   Frankie's grandfather settled himself at the table next to Frankie's grandmother. As his grandparents watched, Frankie returned to his work weeding the tomatoes. Some of the weeds had long roots, and Frankie needed to dig more deeply to pull them out. Suddenly, Frankie's hoe struck something hard. It sounded like something made of metal. Frankie knelt down and tried to pry the object out of the soil. It was a small metal box! Frankie brushed the dirt off the box and showed it to his grandparents. Frankie's grandfather scratched his head and said, "I wonder . . ."

7   Frankie's grandfather's hands trembled a little bit as he held the old box. The grandfather shook his head and said, "I can't believe it." He pointed to the top of the box, where his name, Vince, had been painted in red many, many years ago. "I thought it was lost forever."

8   "Open it up, open it up!" Frankie said. When Frankie's grandfather opened the lid, small paper packets tumbled out and fell into his lap. "Oh, my!" he exclaimed. The seed packets were faded, but Frankie saw the faint outline of a tomato printed on the front of the packets. Frankie's grandfather slowly tore open one of the packets and shook the seeds into the palm of his hand. Tears rolled down his cheeks as he said, "These were the seeds my father brought to America from Italy."

9   "Do you think they'd still grow if we planted them?" Frankie asked. Frankie's grandfather raised his eyebrows and said, "We could try. They've kept dry inside the packets in the metal box." Frankie's grandfather leapt to his feet and grabbed the garden hoe from Frankie, exclaiming, "Let's get back to the gardening!"

ZOOM IN

A detail in the fourth sentence of paragraph 8 can be used as a clue to figure out what kind of seeds were probably inside the paper packets.

■   *Underline this detail clue in the fourth sentence of paragraph 8.*

MY NOTES

Choose the correct answer to each question. Fill in the answer bubble.

1. **At the beginning of the story, detail clues suggest that Frankie was feeling**

   Ⓐ bored.
   Ⓑ angry.
   Ⓒ cold and hungry.
   Ⓓ hot and thirsty.

3. **Detail clues suggest that before Frankie's grandfather joined them, Frankie's grandmother was probably trying to**

   Ⓐ reassure Frankie.
   Ⓑ criticize Frankie's garden work.
   Ⓒ get Frankie to drink more lemonade.
   Ⓓ let Frankie know that she was worried about his grandfather.

2. **Detail clues in the story suggest that Frankie's grandfather grew**

   Ⓐ many kinds of flowers.
   Ⓑ prize-winning tomatoes.
   Ⓒ only beans and squash.
   Ⓓ a variety of tomatoes.

4. **When Frankie's grandfather said that he didn't want Frankie upsetting the tomatoes, the grandfather was probably**

   Ⓐ warning Frankie.
   Ⓑ teasing Frankie.
   Ⓒ instructing Frankie.
   Ⓓ punishing Frankie.

Read why each answer choice is correct or not correct.

1. **Ⓐ not correct**

   Details at the beginning of the story suggest that Frankie thought that gardening was a lot of work, but not that he felt bored.

   Ⓑ not correct

   Details in paragraph 1 suggest that Frankie felt a bit frustrated, but not angry.

   Ⓒ not correct

   Details in paragraph 1 suggest that Frankie felt hot, not cold. Detail clues also suggest that Frankie felt thirsty, not hungry.

   ● correct

   Detail clues in the first three sentences in paragraph 1 suggest that Frankie felt hot and thirsty. He wiped sweat off his forehead, his mouth felt like a wad of dry cotton, and he longed for a sip of cool water.

2. **Ⓐ not correct**

   Flowers are not mentioned in the story.

   Ⓑ not correct

   Details directly state that the grandfather grew tomatoes, but these detail clues do not suggest that the tomatoes had won any prizes.

   Ⓒ not correct

   Details mention beans, but not squash. Many detail clues tell about tomatoes, so Frankie's grandfather did not grow only beans.

   ● correct

   Detail clues in the third sentence in the third paragraph list the names of different varieties of tomatoes. From these detail clues, you can draw the conclusion that Frankie's grandfather grew a variety of tomatoes.

3. **● correct**

   Detail clues in paragraph 4 say that Frankie's grandmother told him not to worry, his grandfather was going to be fine and would perk up. These suggest that Frankie's grandmother was probably trying to reassure Frankie about his grandfather.

   Ⓑ not correct

   Details in paragraph 4 say that she thought that Frankie did a good job.

   Ⓒ not correct

   Details in paragraph 4 suggest that Frankie was thirsty for lemonade, but no details suggest that she was trying to get him to drink more.

   Ⓓ not correct

   Details in paragraph 4 do not suggest whether or not she was worried.

4. **Ⓐ not correct**

   No details suggest that the grandfather was warning Frankie about anything.

   ● correct

   Detail clues say the grandfather's eyes sparkled and that he winked and gave a big smile. So the grandfather was probably teasing Frankie.

   Ⓒ not correct

   There are no details that say that the grandfather was trying to instruct Frankie.

   Ⓓ not correct

   Details suggest that the grandfather was happy with Frankie.

Answer each question. Write each answer on the lines.

5. **Tell how you figured out the answer to question 4. What detail clues did you use to figure out the answer?**

_____

_____

_____

6. **Write a sentence using a detail clue from paragraph 8 that tells what kind of seeds were probably inside the paper packets.**

_____

_____

_____

7. **Write a short paragraph to summarize the whole story. Tell only the most important information.**

_____

_____

_____

_____

_____

5. **Sample Answer:**

The grandfather was probably teasing Frankie about upsetting the tomatoes because when the grandfather spoke, his eyes sparkled, he winked, and he smiled at Frankie.

This is a correct answer because it gives specific detail clues that suggested the grandfather was probably teasing Frankie about upsetting the tomatoes.

6. **Sample Answer:**

Tomato seeds were probably inside the paper packets because the faint outline of a tomato was printed on the front of the packets.

This is a correct answer because it tells that there were probably tomato seeds inside the paper packets, based on a detail clue in paragraph 8.

7. **Sample Answer:**

Frankie was weeding his grandfather's garden. His grandfather had been feeling tired lately. The tomatoes were the pride and joy of his grandfather's garden. While weeding the garden, Frankie found an old metal box. Inside were paper packets filled with tomato seeds that Frankie's grandfather had brought to America from Italy.

This is a correct answer because it is a short paragraph that tells the most important information from the story. The paragraph tells in a general way what the whole story is mostly about.

Lesson 3, Part Four, Independent Practice

This passage is a review of a short story. As you read the review, think about information that is directly stated and what is not directly stated.

ZOOM IN

You can use details in the last two sentences in paragraph 1 as clues to figure out whether or not Sheila probably felt sad about moving again.

■ *Underline the last two sentences in paragraph 1.*

MY NOTES

On the Move

1   Have you ever had to move to a new city or state? For some, moving may be an adventure, but not for me. My name is Sheila. Because of my dad's job, our family usually has to move every couple of years. Every time we move, it feels like I'm starting over. I have to go to a new school, and I have to make new friends. As soon as I feel like I belong, then it's usually time for us to move again. This past fall we moved across the country, from New York to California. When I saw the big moving truck outside our house and the stacks of boxes in our front yard, I sat down on the curb and covered my eyes with my hands. I didn't want anyone to see the tears in my eyes.

2   But, a good thing happened on my first day at the new school. My new teacher, Mr. Ortiz, told our class to read "The Circuit," a short story by Francisco Jiménez. I am now telling all my old friends back in New York to read it. When they read about Panchito and how he had to move often with his family, they will understand how I feel.

3   Panchito and his family were farm workers. As the story begins, it was the end of strawberry season. Panchito and his older brother, Roberto, were driving home from the fields with their father. At the peak of the season, they had worked twelve hours a day, seven days a week picking strawberries. Now, they needed to move to another town in California to look for work. All three were quiet on the way home. For Panchito, the thought of having to move brought tears to his eyes, and he could not sleep that night. I understand how Panchito felt.

4   The author includes many details to help the reader picture things in the story. For example, when the family found work in Fresno, they moved into an old garage on the farm where they worked. The garage did not have any windows. The roof was full of holes. The floor was made of dirt. The family quickly did their best to clean the garage and try to make it their home.

ZOOM IN

Details in the fourth sentence of paragraph 3 can be used as clues to figure out whether or not Panchito, his older brother, and his father were hard workers.

- *Underline the fourth sentence of paragraph 3.*

Detail clues in the third, fourth, and fifth sentences of paragraph 4 can be used as clues to figure out something about the garage that was Panchito's family's new home in Fresno.

- *Underline the third, fourth, and fifth sentences in paragraph 4.*

MY NOTES

Details in the third sentence of paragraph 5 can be used as clues to figure out how late Panchito, his older brother, and their father worked.

■ *Underline the third sentence in paragraph 5.*

The fifth and sixth sentences in paragraph 5 include other details you can use as clues to figure out when their work day ended.

■ *Underline the fifth and sixth sentences in paragraph 5.*

MY NOTES

5   On the farm, Panchito, his older brother, and their father picked grapes. Their day began early in the morning. Their day ended when "the mountains . . . reached out and swallowed the sun." This is another example of how the author uses words to help the reader picture something in the story. After the sun went behind the mountains, it was too dark to see and pick the grapes from the vines. Panchito's father told them it was time to quit for the day.

6   After working in the fields, they cleaned up by taking a shower with a water hose. Panchito's mother made his favorite meal for their dinner. The family ate their dinner at a table made of wooden crates. When it was time for bed, the mother and young children slept on a mattress in the garage. Panchito, Roberto, and their father slept outside under the trees.

7   When it was time for Panchito to go to school, he felt nervous. Once again, I completely understood how he felt. When he got on the school bus for the first time, all the other kids were busy talking and shouting to one another. Panchito sat by himself in a seat at the back of the bus. At the school, a nice lady in the main office helped Panchito get to his classroom.

8   Mr. Lema was Panchito's teacher. He introduced Panchito to the class. Then he asked Panchito if he would like to read from a story the class had already begun. Panchito hesitated. He felt dizzy. He could not begin to read. Mr. Lema told him that it was okay, that he could read later. Then Panchito did something that I'm going to do the next time I have to go to a new school. During recess, Panchito went to see Mr. Lema. He asked Mr. Lema if he would help him learn words he didn't understand. Mr. Lema said, "Gladly." For the next month, Mr. Lema helped Panchito with his reading during the lunch hour.

9   I know Panchito is a character in a story, but I wish we could meet. I think we would understand each other. And I'm hoping my old and new friends will understand me better by reading about Panchito in "The Circuit."

ZOOM IN

Details in the seventh, eleventh, and twelfth sentences of paragraph 8 can be used as clues to figure out whether or not Mr. Lema was probably a kind and thoughtful person.

■ *Underline the seventh, eleventh, and twelfth sentences in paragraph 8.*

MY NOTES

Choose the correct answer to each question. Fill in the answer bubble.

1. **What do detail clues at the beginning of the passage suggest about how Sheila felt about moving?**

   Ⓐ happy
   Ⓑ bored
   Ⓒ sad
   Ⓓ angry

3. **Detail clues suggest that when Panchito's family moved into the garage, it**

   Ⓐ was not in good condition.
   Ⓑ was clean and light.
   Ⓒ had just been built.
   Ⓓ had just been carpeted and painted.

2. **Detail clues suggest that Panchito, his older brother, and their father were probably**

   Ⓐ not used to working long hours.
   Ⓑ hard workers.
   Ⓒ never very busy during the day.
   Ⓓ not hard workers.

4. **How late did Panchito, his older brother, and their father work when picking grapes?**

   Ⓐ until Panchito's mother had dinner ready
   Ⓑ until it got too hot
   Ⓒ until sunset
   Ⓓ until Mr. Sullivan told them to stop

Answer each question. Write each answer on the lines.

5. **Tell how you figured out the answer to question 4. What detail clues did you use to figure out the answer?**

_____

_____

_____

6. **Write a few sentences that tell what kind of person Mr. Lema probably was.**

_____

_____

_____

7. **Write a short paragraph to summarize the review. Tell only the most important information.**

_____

_____

_____

_____

_____

Lesson 4

This passage is a story. As you read the story, think about information that is directly stated and what is not directly stated. Then answer the questions on pages 72 and 73.

MY NOTES

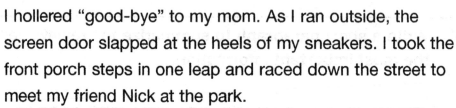

The Day the Sky Turned Green

1   The day began like any normal summer day. After gobbling up my cereal, I slid the bowl across the kitchen counter, making the spoon clatter and spin. I hollered "good-bye" to my mom. As I ran outside, the screen door slapped at the heels of my sneakers. I took the front porch steps in one leap and raced down the street to meet my friend Nick at the park.

2   Nick was already shooting hoops by the time I got there. I must have broken his focus because the basketball hit the metal rim with a loud twang. I laughed as I lunged for the ball and dribbled it down the court. Sweat trickled down both our faces as we tried to block each other's jump shots.

3   After awhile, we stopped to rest. We sat on the grass under the shade of a large oak tree. From there, the clay court almost looked like a big frying pan with the heat sizzling above it.

4   Suddenly, a strong, cool wind came out of nowhere and dried the sweat from our skin, giving us goose bumps. "Whoa, that was weird, Joe." Nick said. As the tree branches swayed above our heads, dark clouds began to form on the horizon.

5   I shivered, but I wasn't cold. The sky had quickly turned yellow, and then it turned an odd shade of green. Not the color of grass or emeralds, but the color of some kind of dangerous monster.

6   All became very quiet and still. Neither of us said a word. We stared at the horizon, our eyes glued to the sight of the dark clouds as they swirled into the form of a black funnel.

7   "Now what do we do?" Nick whispered, his voice cracking. I motioned for him to follow me, and we crawled to the drainage ditch a few feet away. We kept our arms crossed over our heads while what sounded like a freight train roared through the park, snapping tree limbs and tossing picnic tables in the air. Then it was gone.

8   Nick stood up and laughed like nothing had happened. He tossed me the ball, and we picked up where we had left off, shooting baskets and teasing each other about missed shots. The day began and ended like any normal summer day, but we'll always remember it as anything but normal!

Choose the correct answer to each question.

1. **Detail clues at the beginning of the story suggest that**

   Ⓐ Joe thinks the day began in a very strange way.
   Ⓑ Joe is enjoying a slow-paced summer morning.
   Ⓒ Joe is in a hurry to meet his friend at the park.
   Ⓓ Joe's mother isn't at home.

2. **What clue suggests that Nick did not make the basket when Joe first arrived at the park?**

   Ⓐ Nick arrived at the park first to practice shooting baskets.
   Ⓑ The basketball hit the metal rim with a loud twang.
   Ⓒ Sweat trickled down his face as he dribbled the ball.
   Ⓓ The friends tried to block each other's shots.

3. **Why did Joe probably shiver?**

   Ⓐ He was alarmed by the sky turning yellow and green.
   Ⓑ He didn't feel well after shooting baskets.
   Ⓒ He had seen a monster.
   Ⓓ He was cold.

4. **From clues in paragraphs 5 and 6, what kind of storm did Joe and Nick probably experience at the park?**

   Ⓐ a thunderstorm
   Ⓑ a hailstorm
   Ⓒ a flood
   Ⓓ a tornado

Write the answer to each question.

5. **Tell how to figure out the answer to question 4. What passage clues could you use along with what you already know?**

_____

_____

_____

6. **Write a sentence that tells why Joe and Nick probably will always remember the day as anything but normal.**

_____

_____

_____

7. **Write a short paragraph to summarize the story. Tell only the most important information.**

_____

_____

_____

_____

_____

Lesson 5

This passage is a retelling of a fable from India. As you read the fable, think about information that is directly stated and what is not directly stated. Then answer the questions on pages 76 and 77.

MY NOTES

A JAR OF RICE

1   Long ago, in the country of India, there lived a man named Gulam. He lived in the countryside, where most people worked as rice farmers. Gulam's neighbors worked very hard in their rice fields. They planted the grain and tended to the seedlings, hoping for plenty of rain and a good harvest. Gulam could have worked in the rice fields, too. He was young, strong, and healthy. Instead, he sat by the window and daydreamed about becoming rich.

2   One day, Gulam begged one of his neighbors to give him some rice, as he had not worked for his own. The neighbor gave Gulam a small amount of rice, but he shook his head at Gulam. He said, "You should be ashamed of yourself, Gulam."

3   Gulam didn't care what his neighbor or the other villagers thought of him. He was going to become rich, and he wouldn't have to work for his money. He had other ideas.

4   Gulam put the handful of rice from his neighbor into a clay jar and daydreamed about his plans to become wealthy. First, he would plant the grains of rice. Then, after a great harvest, he would store the rice and not sell it right away. He would wait until there was a shortage of food in his country, when people would be very hungry. Then he would sell the rice for a large amount of money.

5   With all this money, Gulam dreamed that he would buy cattle and horses and build many barns and stables. He would marry a beautiful woman and have six sons. He and his family would live in a grand house on a large estate.

6   Gulam was excited about all his dreams. He was most excited about inviting his neighbors over to visit. He would show them all that he had accomplished. Then Gulam imagined, the neighbors would change their minds about him.

7   In his state of excitement, Gulam waved his arms and accidentally knocked the clay jar onto the floor. The jar broke, and the rice spilled out. Before Gulam could pick up the grains of rice, the wind blew them away. Now Gulam was left with nothing. He did not have the cattle, horses, barns, and stables that he'd dreamed of. He did not have a wife and sons. He did not have a house or an estate. He did not even have a single grain of rice.

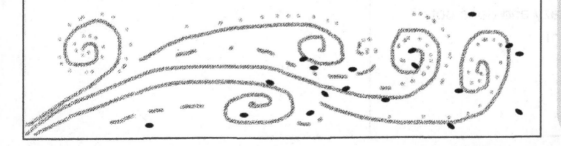

Choose the correct answer to each question.

1. **At the beginning of the fable, detail clues suggest that Gulam is**

   Ⓐ a hardworking farmer.
   Ⓑ a lazy daydreamer.
   Ⓒ a wise villager.
   Ⓓ a rich merchant.

2. **Why does the neighbor probably shake his head at Gulam?**

   Ⓐ because the neighbor thinks Gulam brags and shows off his wealth
   Ⓑ because the neighbor is angry with Gulam for borrowing rice
   Ⓒ because the neighbor likes Gulam and wants him to be successful
   Ⓓ because the neighbor thinks Gulam is lazy and does not respect him

3. **Gulam imagines how he would use the handful of rice from his neighbor to make himself wealthy. From these detail clues, which word best describes Gulam?**

   Ⓐ generous
   Ⓑ fair
   Ⓒ suspicious
   Ⓓ greedy

4. **In paragraph 6, Gulam probably hopes his neighbors will**

   Ⓐ admire him as a wealthy man.
   Ⓑ still think of him as lazy.
   Ⓒ be happy that they no longer have to give him rice.
   Ⓓ want to share his wealth.

5. **From clues in the fable and what you already know about daydreaming and not doing much work, you can draw a conclusion about the lesson that Gulam probably learned. What was the lesson?**

_____

_____

_____

6. **What was it about Gulam's behavior that caused him to end up with nothing? Your behavior is how you act, what you do or don't do.**

_____

_____

_____

7. **Write a short paragraph to summarize the fable. Tell only the most important information.**

_____

_____

_____

_____

_____

Lesson 6

This passage is a report. As you read the report, think about information that is directly stated and what is not directly stated. Then answer the questions on pages 80 and 81.

FRIGHTENING FANGS!

1   Picture these creatures. A rattlesnake slithers across a sandy desert. A tarantula with long, hairy legs crawls along the leaf-littered ground. A vampire bat flies with outstretched wings in the moonlit night. What do these different creatures have in common? Fangs!

2   Fangs are long, sharp teeth. Animals use their fangs to capture and eat prey. Without fangs, some animals would not be able to get food. Animals also use fangs to protect and defend themselves from enemies. Some scientists think that as some animals evolved, they grew fangs as a special physical trait, or feature.

3   There are three categories, or classes, of fanged animals. The first class of animals has fangs in the back of their mouth. The second class has fangs in the front of their mouth. The third class has fangs in the front, which fold back into their mouth. With their fangs, some of these animals inject venom into their victims.

4   Rattlesnakes inject venom into their prey through both fangs. The venom is a powerful poison. It quickly kills the prey. It also helps to break down the victim's body. The victim's

body becomes soft. Then the rattlesnake swallows it. Rattlesnakes will attack people. However, they attack only when they are disturbed or threatened. Rattlesnake venom is so powerful that it can kill an adult human in less than an hour. When not in use, a rattlesnake's front fangs fold back into its mouth.

5   Tarantulas also inject venom through both fangs. Their fangs are larger than those of some snakes. Tarantulas, however, look scarier than

they really are. For the most part, they are not dangerous to people. A tarantula bite can cause a person great pain. It is not fatal, however. A tarantula's prey includes crickets, grasshoppers, and beetles.

6   Vampire bats have razor-sharp fangs. They use their fangs to bite their victims. They do this while their victims are asleep. Then the bats lick the blood from the bite wound. Blood is the only food in this type of bat's diet. Usually, they bite large animals such as horses and cows. They bite people, too. The bite itself is not dangerous. However, vampire bats carry rabies. Rabies is a very dangerous disease. People fear this tiny bat because of the risk of getting rabies.

Choose the correct answer to each question.

1. **At the beginning of the report, detail clues suggest that**

   Ⓐ only rattlesnakes have fangs.
   Ⓑ only tarantulas have fangs.
   Ⓒ a variety of animals have fangs.
   Ⓓ rattlesnakes, tarantulas, and vampire bats have nothing in common.

2. **From detail clues in paragraph 2, you can figure out that**

   Ⓐ animals use their fangs only to capture prey.
   Ⓑ fangs help some animals survive.
   Ⓒ fangs serve no special purpose for animals.
   Ⓓ scientists do not understand why certain animals grew fangs as they evolved.

3. **There are three classes of fanged animals, and you can figure out from detail clues that rattlesnakes**

   Ⓐ belong to the first class of fanged animals.
   Ⓑ belong to the second class of fanged animals.
   Ⓒ belong to the third class of fanged animals.
   Ⓓ do not have fangs.

4. **From the report, you can figure out that**

   Ⓐ tarantula bites are the most dangerous to humans because of the large fangs.
   Ⓑ rattlesnake bites are never fatal to humans.
   Ⓒ vampire bat bites are worse than rattlesnake bites.
   Ⓓ rattlesnake bites are the most dangerous to humans.

Write the answer to each question.

5. **Tell why vampire bats probably would not survive without their fangs.**

_____

_____

_____

6. **Tell how vampire bats probably got their name.**

_____

_____

_____

7. **Write a short paragraph to summarize the report. Tell only the most important information.**

_____

_____

_____

_____

_____

Lesson 7

This passage is an article. As you read the article, think about information that is directly stated and what is not directly stated. Then answer the questions on pages 84 and 85.

Why Does It Feel Good to Laugh?

1   When you hear a group of friends laughing, what do you do? Chances are good that you approach them and ask, "What's so funny?" People are naturally drawn to the sound of laughter. One person starts to laugh, and soon everyone is laughing. Even if they're laughing at a corny joke, people feel good when they laugh. If laughter feels so good, could it have health benefits as well? The old saying "laughter is the best medicine" might prove to be true after all.

2   Laughter has many effects on the body. Enjoying a hearty laugh lowers a person's blood pressure and protects the heart. A good, hearty laugh affects the brain in a positive way. Think about the way your body moves when you laugh. These movements exercise muscles in the face, stomach, lungs, and back. Hearty laughter also burns calories!

3   Laughter has many effects on the mind. It relaxes people. It reduces stress. It boosts people's moods. Laughter encourages people to talk more with one another. People also make more eye contact when they are laughing. Laughter gets rid of negative emotions, such as anger or sadness. Laughter replaces them with positive emotions, such as joy or happiness. Laughter may not solve life's problems. It does, however, help to keep them in their place.

4   The ability to laugh begins at a very early age. During the first weeks of life, babies begin to smile. Within a few months, they are able to laugh out loud. People, therefore, are born with the gift of laughter. As people grow older, though, they often laugh less. Sometimes, they even lose their sense of humor.

5   So, how do people bring more laughter into their daily lives? They can begin by smiling. When one person smiles, other people smile in response. Soon, a smile can bubble up into a laugh. When people hear laughter, they should move toward it. Smiles and laughter are best when shared with others. Laughter offers many benefits to people. To stay healthy, people need exercise and good food. One day, doctors may also prescribe a daily dose of laughter.

MY NOTES

Choose the correct answer to each question.

1. **In paragraph 1, what clue suggests that laughter is contagious, or catching?**

   Ⓐ Someone asks, "What's so funny?"
   Ⓑ One person starts to laugh, and soon everyone is laughing.
   Ⓒ People feel good when they laugh.
   Ⓓ Laughter is the best medicine.

2. **Why does laughter probably give a person's body a great workout?**

   Ⓐ because it lowers a person's blood pressure
   Ⓑ because it exercises muscles in the face, stomach, lungs, and back and burns calories
   Ⓒ because it affects the brain in a positive way
   Ⓓ because it protects the heart

3. **Detail clues in the article suggest that**

   Ⓐ laughter solves life's problems.
   Ⓑ laughter increases negative emotions.
   Ⓒ laughter creates a barrier between people.
   Ⓓ laughter helps people to connect with one another.

4. **From the article, you can figure out that**

   Ⓐ laughter has many healthy effects on people's bodies and minds.
   Ⓑ laughter is developed later in life, when people are adults.
   Ⓒ laughter is best enjoyed when a person is alone.
   Ⓓ laughter is better for people's health than exercise and good food.

5. Tell how to figure out the answer to question 2. What passage clues did you use?

_____

_____

_____

6. Write a sentence that tells why people should try to laugh more often.

_____

_____

_____

7. Write a short paragraph to summarize the article. Tell only the most important information.

_____

_____

_____

_____

_____

_____

Lesson 8

This passage is a review. As you read the review, think about information that is directly stated and what is not directly stated. Then answer the questions on pages 88 and 89.

MY NOTES

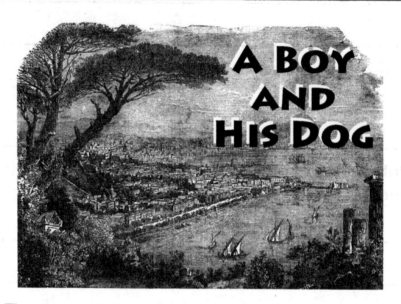

A BOY AND HIS DOG

1   The connection between humans and dogs has fascinated people for a long time. It is a common theme in books. I've read many stories that have this theme. One of my favorite stories with this theme is "The Dog of Pompeii," by Louis Untermeyer. It takes place in an ancient time. Readers of all ages can relate to the story, which tells about a friendship between a blind boy and his dog. Read this story, and I promise you'll never forget Tito and his dog Bimbo.

2   As the story begins, Tito and Bimbo are waking up to a new day. They live in Pompeii. It was a city in the Roman Empire. The author did a very good job creating the setting of the story. The reader quickly experiences the sights and sounds of the city. Shining chariots race through the streets. Crowds gather in open-air theaters. Fireworks burst in the air for days when the Roman emperor comes to visit once a year.

3   The author created two very convincing main characters. Many details tell the reader about Tito and Bimbo. For example, Tito and Bimbo live on the streets and sleep under the wall of the city's inner gate. Tito has been blind since birth. The dog Bimbo leaves Tito's side only three times a day. When Bimbo returns, he brings food for them to eat. Sometimes their meal is a scrap of meat or a piece of fruit. Sometimes it is a flat cake with raisins and sugar. This is Tito's favorite. With Bimbo's care, Tito never goes hungry.

4   The plot of the story develops further when Tito and Bimbo go to the forum. The forum is where the people of Pompeii gather to hear and talk about the latest news. At the forum, Tito hears a stranger issue a warning. He warns everyone about a thick column of smoke. It is pouring out from the top of Mount Vesuvius.

5   The next morning, Bimbo urgently pulls Tito to his feet. Tito cannot see what is happening, but he senses a change. The author uses vivid details to help the reader hear and feel what Tito hears and feels. For example, Tito hears strange sounds. It sounds as if animals are under the earth. Tito also feels the ground twitching. Suddenly, red-hot ashes burn his skin. Toxic fumes tear at his throat. What is happening? Is Bimbo able to save Tito? You'll have to read the story to find out!

Choose the correct answer to each question.

1. **From detail clues at the beginning of the review, you can figure out that the story's theme is**

   Ⓐ not very interesting.
   Ⓑ a new trend.
   Ⓒ uncommon.
   Ⓓ timeless.

3. **In paragraph 3, detail clues suggest that**

   Ⓐ Tito has wealthy parents.
   Ⓑ Tito and Bimbo do not trust each other.
   Ⓒ Tito probably could not survive without Bimbo.
   Ⓓ Everyone in Pompeii helps care for Tito.

2. **From detail clues in the review, you can figure out that**

   Ⓐ Pompeii is a lively city.
   Ⓑ Pompeii is a boring village.
   Ⓒ Pompeii is the center of the Roman Empire.
   Ⓓ Pompeii is where the Roman emperor lives.

4. **By the end of the review, you can figure out that**

   Ⓐ Mount Vesuvius has probably erupted.
   Ⓑ Fireworks are probably on display for the emperor.
   Ⓒ An earthquake has probably struck Pompeii.
   Ⓓ Pompeii has probably come under surprise attack.

Write the answer to each question.

5. **Write two sentences that describe the relationship between Tito and Bimbo.**

_____

_____

_____

6. **Write a sentence that tells why the reviewer probably thinks that others will want to read this story.**

_____

_____

_____

7. **Write a short paragraph to summarize the review. Tell only the most important information.**

_____

_____

_____

_____

_____

TRACKING CHART

Name_____

Write the date under **Date Completed** *after you have completed the Introduction, each part, and each lesson. After questions have been corrected, fill in the number that you answered correctly under* **Questions Correct**. *After you have completed each lesson, complete a Self-Assessment.*

	Date Completed	Questions Correct
Introduction		
Lesson 1		
Part One, Modeled Instruction		
Part Two, Guided Instruction		
Part Three, Guided Practice		/7
Part Four, Independent Practice		/7
Now complete Self-Assessment 1, for Lesson 1.		
Lesson 2		
Part One, Modeled Instruction		
Part Two, Guided Instruction		
Part Three, Guided Practice		/7
Part Four, Independent Practice		/7
Now complete Self-Assessment 2, for Lesson 2.		
Lesson 3		
Part One, Modeled Instruction		
Part Two, Guided Instruction		
Part Three, Guided Practice		/7
Part Four, Independent Practice		/7
Now complete Self-Assessment 3, for Lesson 3.		
Lesson 4		
Now complete Self-Assessment 4, for Lesson 4.		/7
Lesson 5		
Now complete Self-Assessment 5, for Lesson 5.		/7
Lesson 6		
Now complete Self-Assessment 6, for Lesson 6.		/7
Lesson 7		
Now complete Self-Assessment 7, for Lesson 7.		/7
Lesson 8		
Now complete Self-Assessment 8, for Lesson 8.		/7

SELF-ASSESSMENT 1

Name_____ **Date**_____

Answer these questions after you have completed Lesson 1.

1. Rate your work in Lesson 1. Circle your answer.

    successful   somewhat successful   needs improvement

2. Did any of the reading passages or questions give you trouble? _____
   If so, what kind of trouble did you have?

   _____

   _____

3. Complete this sentence. *I could have done even better in Lesson 1 if*

   _____

   _____

   _____

   _____

   _____.

4. What is your goal for Lesson 2?

   _____

   _____

SELF-ASSESSMENT 2

Name_____ **Date**_____

Answer these questions after you have completed Lesson 2.

1. Rate your work in Lesson 2. Circle your answer.

    successful   somewhat successful   needs improvement

2. Did any of the reading passages or questions give you trouble? _____
   If so, what kind of trouble did you have?

   _____

   _____

   Is this the same kind of trouble you had in Lesson 1? _____

3. Did you find the reading passages or questions easier or more difficult than
   those in Lesson 1?

   _____

   Why do you think this is so?

   _____

   _____

4. Did you meet the goal you set for yourself for Lesson 2?_____
   Why or why not?

   _____

   _____

5. What is your goal for Lesson 3?

   _____

   _____

 Drawing Conclusions and Making Inferences, Book D

SELF-ASSESSMENT 3

Name_____ **Date**_____

Answer these questions after you have completed Lesson 3.

1. Rate your work in Lesson 3. Circle your answer.

   successful   somewhat successful   needs improvement

2. Did any of the reading passages or questions give you trouble? _____
   If so, what kind of trouble did you have?

   _____

   _____

   Is this the same kind of trouble you had in Lesson 2? _____

3. Did you find the reading passages or questions easier or more difficult than
   those in Lesson 2?

   _____

   Why do you think this is so?

   _____

   _____

4. Did you meet the goal you set for yourself for Lesson 3?_____
   Why or why not?

   _____

   _____

5. Complete this sentence: *I could have done even better in Lessons 1–3 if*

   _____

   _____.

Name_____ **Date**_____

Answer these questions after you have completed Lesson 4.

1. Rate your work in Lesson 4. Circle your answer.

    successful   somewhat successful   needs improvement

2. Did any of the reading passages or questions give you trouble? _____
    If so, what kind of trouble did you have?

    _____

    _____

3. Complete this sentence: *I could have done even better in Lesson 4 if*

    _____

    _____

    _____

    _____

    _____ .

4. What is your goal for Lesson 5?

    _____

    _____

SELF-ASSESSMENT 5

Name_____ **Date**_____

Answer these questions after you have completed Lesson 5.

1. Rate your work in Lesson 5. Circle your answer.

   successful   somewhat successful   needs improvement

2. Did any of the reading passages or questions give you trouble? _____
   If so, what kind of trouble did you have?

   _____

   _____

   Is this the same kind of trouble you had in Lesson 4? _____

3. Did you find the reading passages or questions easier or more difficult than
   those in Lesson 4?

   _____

   Why do you think this is so?

   _____

   _____

4. Did you meet the goal you set for yourself for Lesson 5?_____
   Why or why not?

   _____

   _____

5. What is your goal for Lesson 6?

   _____

   _____

SELF-ASSESSMENT 6

Name_____ **Date**_____

Answer these questions after you have completed Lesson 6.

1. Rate your work in Lesson 6. Circle your answer.

    successful   somewhat successful   needs improvement

2. Did any of the reading passages or questions give you trouble? _____
    If so, what kind of trouble did you have?

    _____

    _____

    Is this the same kind of trouble you had in Lesson 5? _____

3. Did you find the reading passages or questions easier or more difficult than
    those in Lesson 5?

    _____

    Why do you think this is so?

    _____

    _____

4. Did you meet the goal you set for yourself for Lesson 6?_____
    Why or why not?

    _____

    _____

5. What is your goal for Lesson 7?

    _____

    _____

 Drawing Conclusions and Making Inferences, Book D

SELF-ASSESSMENT 7

Name_____ **Date**_____

Answer these questions after you have completed Lesson 7.

1. Rate your work in Lesson 7. Circle your answer.

   successful   somewhat successful   needs improvement

2. Did any of the reading passages or questions give you trouble? _____
   If so, what kind of trouble did you have?

   _____

   _____

   Is this the same kind of trouble you had in Lesson 6? _____

3. Did you find the reading passages or questions easier or more difficult than
   those in Lesson 6?

   _____

   Why do you think this is so?

   _____

   _____

4. Did you meet the goal you set for yourself for Lesson 7?_____
   Why or why not?

   _____

   _____

5. What is your goal for Lesson 8?

   _____

   _____

SELF-ASSESSMENT 8

Name_____ **Date**_____

Answer these questions after you have completed Lesson 8.

1. Rate your work in Lesson 8. Circle your answer.

   successful   somewhat successful   needs improvement

2. Did any of the reading passages or questions give you trouble? _____
   If so, what kind of trouble did you have?

   _____

   _____

   Is this the same kind of trouble you had in Lesson 7? _____

3. Did you find the reading passages or questions easier or more difficult than
   those in Lesson 7?

   _____

   Why do you think this is so?

   _____

   _____

4. Did you meet the goal you set for yourself for Lesson 8? _____
   Why or why not?

   _____

   _____

5. Complete this sentence: *I could have done even better in Lessons 4–8 if*

   _____

   _____.

Name_____ **Date**_____

Clues in Passage	**What You Already Know**	**Conclusion or Inference**
	+	→

Photo and Illustration Credits